GRAND HOMES
OF THE SOUTH

Text by Bill Harris

Editor
Gillian Waugh

Commissioning Editor
Trevor Hall

Designer
Philip Clucas MSIAD

Photography
Chris Swan, Ric Pattison and Andrew Heaps

Production Director
Gerald Hughes

Editorial Director
David Gibbon

Publishing Director
Ted Smart

CLB 853

Published 1987 by Crescent Books,
Distributed by Crown Publishers, Inc.
ISBN 0 517 478129
h g f e d c b a
Dop. Leg. B.17289-87

GRAND HOMES OF THE SOUTH

Text by
BILL HARRIS

CRESCENT BOOKS
NEW YORK

"The house had been built according to no architectural plan whatever, with extra rooms added where and when it seemed convenient, but, with care and attention, it gained a charm that made up for its lack of design. The avenue of cedars, leading from the main road to the house – that avenue of cedars without which no Georgia planter's home could be complete – had a cool dark shadiness that gave a brighter tinge, by contrast, to the green of the other trees. The wistaria tumbling over the verandahs showed bright against the whitewashed brick and it joined with the pink crepe myrtle bushes by the door and the white-blossomed magnolias in the yard to disguise some of the awkward lines of the house."

Of all the great homes of the South, the one those words describe is probably the best known. It is the house that comes to mind almost immediately the mind's eye turns south of the Mason-Dixon line. But it is a house that doesn't exist. It was created in 1936 by Margaret Mitchell, along with Scarlett O'Hara and Rhett Butler, for her classic *Gone With The Wind.*

"Tara," as she called it, is a composite of hundreds of plantation houses that existed before the Civil War in the Old South from Virginia to Florida and west to the Mississippi River, and is as fitting a symbol of the South as any one of them. But the great homes of the South come in other forms, too. Symbolic of some of those is the house in Savannah that had been the girlhood home of Scarlett O'Hara's mother, also described in *Gone With The Wind:*

"She had left a home whose lines were as beautiful and flowing as a woman's body, a ship in full sail; a pale pink stucco house built in the French Colonial style, set high from the ground in a dainty manner, approached by swirling stairs, bannistered with wrought iron, delicate as lace; a dim, rich house, graceful but aloof."

Grace. Even a house that might be considered awkward in any other setting takes on a kind of grace in the southern United States. It was like that from the very beginning, when the settlers of Jamestown, Virginia, brought English tradition to the New World and modified it to suit the new landscape. The Georgian style, fashionable in the Old World at the time, was a symbol of elegance to the Virginia Cavaliers and their plantation houses followed the style with only minor changes, such as broad center halls, to suit the demands of the climate. For a century and a half, Georgian was the only style that mattered to anyone who wanted to present an image of good taste and gentility. And the image moved down the coast as well as west, pushing aside French and Spanish influences.

In England, the style had been executed in brick and stone. But here in America, the building material of choice was usually wood, which was available in such abundance. Local brick was generally too soft to make the proper statement, but when a planter really wanted to impress his neighbors, brick or stone was the best way to do it, no matter how far he had to go to get it. Eventually, of course, brick became more common, and planters in search of better status symbols began adding wide verandahs to their homes for outdoor entertaining, and another element that would become a symbol of the South moved America another step away from Mother England.

In the mid-17th century, another country was heard from when Charleston, South Carolina, became the largest city south of Philadelphia. The Carolinians weren't as bound to English tradition as their neighbors up in Virginia and, though they also wanted their houses to make an impression on their neighbors, many of those neighbors were French and quite pointedly unimpressed by things English. Thanks to the new prejudice, or lack of it, graceful wrought iron became part of the scene. The Virginian verandah seemed like a good idea, so they adopted it, or rather improved on it, by building two-story porches overlooking the private gardens at the side of their townhouses.

They also changed the style of living. Up in Virginia it had become customary for people who mattered to live all year in elegant plantation houses, leaving the towns as places for tradesmen and the rest of the middle class. In South Carolina, the image of the country gentleman with his vast estate wasn't considered as important and the gentry was more than happy to live in close proximity to other people, leaving us a legacy of some of the finest townhouses anywhere in America.

A half century later, new architectural ideas arrived from England when the Georgia colony was established at Savannah. Its founder, James Oglethorpe, had it all worked out on paper long before he left home. In the years since the future Virginians first left England in 1607, ideas had changed and the emphasis had moved to town planning. By 1733, when Oglethorpe decided to leave, English ideas for better living had been refined enough to give America its first

major city with broad, orderly streets and an open square every two blocks. Though the colonies in the North had grown up around cities like Boston, Philadelphia and New York, the Southern tradition, until Savannah and Charleston, was content to wait until cities could be made liveable.

The notable exception to the rule is the city of New Orleans, which from the very beginning has had traditions all its own. The French and Spanish were there first and held no brief with any ideas imported from Great Britain. Unlike the English, they had experience back home with sub-tropical climates and the architecture they brought with them was already well-adapted to it. Like other immigrants to America, they refined the style and reshaped it to fit, but in the process they never hid their roots, giving us a city that is totally different from any other in the country.

But the popular image of the Old South isn't in its cities, in spite of their charm, but in the magnificent, romantic old plantation houses built in the Greek Revival style that spread from the South to the rest of the country in the first half of the 19th century. The pattern was established by Thomas Jefferson, who began building his Monticello at Charlottesville, Virginia, in 1772. Jefferson, a man as accomplished in architecture as anyone of his time, had shrugged off the popular Georgian style of the day as elitist and decided that the only true form of architecture was developed in ancient Rome and resurrected by the 16th-century Italian Andrea Palladio. He softened his views after going abroad in 1784 and discovering a Greek temple in Southern France. "I gazed at it whole hours, like a lover at his mistress," he said later.

He brought the love home with him and infected his neighbors with it. Classical order in buildings and gardens became fashionable, and the environment created over the next half-century has become one of the South's great contributions to our civilization. That great era of building came to a crashing halt when the Civil War broke out, and during the poverty-stricken generations following the war time stood still. In the absence of what we Americans think of as "progress," the houses that survived the war were protected for us, and the legacy of an earlier time, another way of life, is still there to stir the imagination.

Is there anyone who has stood in front of one of those big houses and not imagined frail and delicate young women in wide hoop skirts and crinolines flirting with earnest young men in fashionable waistcoats? In your mind's eye, you can see the squire of the estate sitting there on the verandah with his wife, both fashionably dressed, both benignly proud of what they have accomplished, and both pleased to share their bounty with you.

It's a beautiful image, and, to be sure, there were some cotton plantations where the scene was played out time and again in the antebellum South. But in spite of their elegant houses, the majority of Southern planters were farmers with huge tracts of land to manage. They had slaves to help, of course, but their lives were full of hard work and even harder responsibility. Possibly more typical of the 19th-century Southern plantation owner than any movie or novel will tell you is the one landscape architect Frederick Law Olmstead described in his 1860 *Journey in the Back Country*. The man owned dozens of slaves, had extensive herds of cattle, and lived in the best house for many miles around. But he didn't own a pair of shoes. His wife smoked a pipe. Neither of them could read very well, but spent long hours each evening sounding out words in the family Bible. Because of their isolation in the Tennessee back country, their speech patterns had degenerated to the dialect of their field hands.

But their house was a substantial three stories with a two-story verandah. There was a fireplace in every room, a huge center hall to give the right impression to visitors, and a stairway that made it even more impressive. It was the showplace of the plantation that included neat barns and stables, a street of slave cabins, a smokehouse and a big detached kitchen where food was sometimes prepared in the same bowls used for washing.

In his world, the squire was one of the landed gentry; a man of substance. But the hard work of managing his estate, the climate and life at the edge of the frontier left him little time to shave off the rough edges. When he had time to relax, he was more likely to enjoy a cigar than a mint julep, and he and his wife entertained their neighbors on a regular basis with evenings of community singing. They never missed church on Sunday, their only day of rest.

Though men like him represented the majority of planters, there was an aristocracy in the Old South and it was something to aspire to among the sons of the pioneer planters. As Scarlett O'Hara said, their goal was "raising good cotton, riding well, shooting straight, dancing lightly, squiring the ladies with elegance and carrying one's liquor with elegance." And, indeed, many plantation houses boasted fine libraries stocked with the classics. Some planters could even read them, though few seem to have bothered. A reporter from Britain who toured the

South in 1860 wrote that "they afford ample occupation for a rainy day."

New Yorker George Templeton Strong, whose opinion was tempered by Northern provincialism, wrote in his diary that "...a rich Southern aristocrat is of fine nature with the self-reliance and high tone that life among the aristocracy favors, and culture and polish from books and travel strikes us as something different from ourselves, more ornamental and in some respects better. He has the polish of a highly civilized society with the qualities that belong to a ruler of serfs. Thus a notion has gotten footing here that the 'Southern gentlemen' are a high-bred chivalric society, something like Louis XIV's noblesse, with grave faults, to be sure, but on the whole very gallant and generous, regulating themselves by 'codes of honor' (that are wrong, of course, but very grand), not rich but surrounded by all the elements of real refinement."

The elements of "real refinement" are alive and well in the great homes of the South. And if the people who lived in them defy being placed in convenient common niches, the quality of their lives comes through to us in the places they lived, the gardens they strolled, the fields they oversaw.

The spirit of Romanticism was sweeping the country in the early 19th century when the Old South was in full flower, and it is preserved for us in the South more than anywhere else in the United States. And no other part of the United States offers more opportunities to revisit the past in as many beautiful mansions restored as museums. They are places where time is standing still and providing all of us with an opportunity to examine a pace that unfortunately seems to have eluded us in the last half of the 20th century. It's why so many Americans agree with the old song that says, "I wish I were in the land of cotton, Old times there are not forgotten."

Visitor's Guide

Many of the homes and gardens in these pages may be visited. The following is a selection of some of them.

Alabama

Arlington, 331 Cotton Avenue SW, Birmingham (205-780-5656). Open daily except Monday and major holidays. Admission charge. Handicapped facilities.

Bluff Hall, 405 N. Commissioners Street, Demopolis (205-289-1666). Open daily except Monday and major holidays. Admission charge. Includes a clothing museum and craft shop.

Fort Conde-Charlotte House, 104 Theatre Street, Mobile (205-438-7304). Closed Mondays and major holidays, including Mardi Gras Day. Free.

Gaineswood, 805 South Cedar Street, Demopolis (205-289-4846). Open daily except major holidays. Admission charge.

Gorgas House, Ninth Avenue and Capstone Drive, Tuscaloosa (205-348-6010). Open daily except holidays. The museum includes a collection of Spanish Colonial silver. Free.

Oakleigh, 350 Oakleigh Place, Mobile (205-432-1281). Closed holidays, Mardi Gras and Christmas week. Admission charge.

Richards-DAR House, 256 N. Joachim Street, Mobile (205-438-7320). Open daily except major holidays. Admission charge.

Sturdivant Hall, 713 Mabry Street, Selma (205-872-1377). Closed Mondays and holidays. Admission charge includes a one-hour guided tour.

Arkansas

McCollum-Chidester House, 926 Washington Street, Camden (501-836-9243). Open May through October, except Saturdays. Admission charge includes a tour of the house and of the nearby 1850 Leake-Ingham Building.

Rosalie House, 282 Spring Street, Eureka Springs (501-253-7411). Open from mid-March through mid-November and by appointment. Admission charge.

Florida

Ringling Museums, U.S. Highway 41, Sarasota (813-351-1600). Open daily. Handicapped facilities. The admission charge includes the Ringling Residence, Ca'd'zan, the Museum of Art, the Asolo Theater, the Museum of the Circus and the rose garden.

Georgia

Isaiah Davenport House, 324 East State Street, Savannah (912-236-8097). Open daily except holidays. Admission charge.

Lapham-Patterson House Historic Site, 626 North Dawson Street, Thomasville (912-226-0405). Open daily except Monday and holidays. The admission charge includes a guided tour.

Andrew Low House, 329 Abercorn Street, Savannah (912-233-6854). Open daily except Thursday and major holidays. Admission charge.

Juliette Gordon Low Birthplace, 142 Bull Street, Savannah (912-233-4501). Open daily except Wednesday and holidays and on Sunday February through November. Admission charge.

Pebble Hill Plantation, U.S. 319, Thomasville (912-226-2344). Open daily except Monday. Children are not permitted in the Main House, but are welcome on the grounds, which include a dog hospital and a carriage collection. Admission charge.

Susina Plantation, Route 3, Thomasville (912-377-9644) is open as an inn and includes a swimming pool, tennis courts and a stocked fishing pond.

Kentucky

Ashland, Richmond Road at Sycamore Street, Lexington (606-266-8581). Open daily except Christmas Day. Admission charge.

Farmington, 3033 Bardstown Road, Louisville (502-452-9920). Open daily except holidays, including Derby Day. Admission charge.

My Old Kentucky Home, U.S. 150, Bardstown (502-348-3502). Open daily April through October, closed Mondays at other times of the year. The admission fee for the house includes a tour guided by attendants in period costumes. The grounds, a state park, are free.

White Hall State Shrine, Richmond (606-623-9178). Open daily April through Labor Day and Wednesday through Sunday from Labor Day to October. Admission charge.

Louisiana

Ashland-Belle Helene Plantation, River Road at Ashland Road, Baton Rouge (504-473-8135). Open daily. Admission charge.

Destrehan Plantation, Route 48, Destrehan (504-764-9315). Open daily except major holidays. Admission charge includes a guided tour.

Glencoe, Route 68, Jackson (504-629-5387). Open daily except major holidays. Admission charge includes a guided tour. Some overnight accommodations available.

Hermann-Grima House, 820 St. Louis Street, New Orleans (504-525-5661). Open daily except Sunday and holidays. Creole cooking demonstrations are given on Thursdays from October through May. Admission charge.

Houmas House, River Road, Burnside (504-473-7481). Open daily except major holidays. Admission charge includes a guided tour.

Madewood, Route 2, Napoleonville (504-369-7151). Open daily except Christmas and Thanksgiving. Overnight accommodations available. Admission charge includes a guided tour.

Nottoway Plantation, Route 1, Baton Rouge (504-545-2730). Open daily except Christmas day. Overnight accommodations and restaurant facilities are available. Admission charge.

Oak Alley Plantation, Great River Road, Vacherie (504-256-2151). Open daily except New Year's day, Thanksgiving and Christmas days. Handicapped facilities, picnic grounds, restaurant. Admission charge.

Rosedown, Route 10, Baton Rouge. Open daily except major holidays. Admission charge.

San Francisco Plantation, Garyville (504-535-2341). Open daily except major holidays. Admission charge.

Mississippi

Cedar Grove, 2200 Oak Street, Vicksburg (601-636-1605). Open daily. Overnight accommodations available. Admission charge includes a guided tour.

Dunleith, 84 Homochito Street, Natchez (601-446-8500). Open daily except Thanksgiving and Christmas days. Overnight accommodations with breakfast. Admission charge.

The Natchez Pilgrimage Association (800-647-6743) sponsors tours of more than 30 historic homes in the spring and fall each year.

Rosalie, 100 Orleans Street, Natchez (601-445-4555). Open daily, closed December 24 and 25. Admission charge.

Waverley Plantation, Route 50, West Point (601-494-1399). Open daily. Admission charge.

North Carolina

Arlie Gardens, Wrightsville Beach Highway, Wilmington. Open daily except holidays. The entrance fee is for the gardens only. The house is not open.

Biltmore Estate, Asheville (704-274-1776). Open daily except New Year's, Thanksgiving and Christmas days. Fifty-five of the 255 rooms in the house are open for viewing as are the 35 acres of formal gardens. Restaurant facilities, winery. Admission charge.

The North Carolina Azalea Festival is held at Wilmington in early April. Information is available through the Chamber of Commerce, 514 Market Street, Wilmington (919-762-2611).

Orton Plantation Gardens, Route 133, Wilmington (919-371-6851). Open daily, March through November. Admission charge is for the gardens only. The house is not open.

Tyron Palace and Gardens, 610 Pollack Street, New Bern (919-638-1560). Open daily except January 1, Thanksgiving and December 24 and 25. Guided tours are by hostesses in costume. Admission charge.

South Carolina

Boone Hall Plantation, U.S. 17, Mount Pleasant (803-884-4371). Open every day except Thanksgiving and Christmas days. The admission charge includes the nine original slave houses, the gin house and several restored rooms in the main house.

Cypress Gardens, U.S. 52, Charleston (803-553-0515). Open every day.
Admission charge. Children free.

Drayton Hall, Route 4, Charleston (803-766-0188). Open daily except New Year's, Thanksgiving and Christmas days. Admission fee includes a guided tour. Children free.

Heyward-Washington House, 87 Church Street, Charleston. Open daily except holidays. Admission charge includes the Joseph Manigault House, 350 Meeting Street, and the Aiken-Rhett Mansion, 48 Elizabeth Street.

The Historic Beaufort Foundation, P.O. Box 11, Beaufort (803-524-6334) sponsors tours of the town's historic homes and gardens in mid-April.

Historic Charleston Foundation, 51 Meeting Street (803-722-3405) sponsors a Festival of Houses in late March and early April. Many homes are open for afternoon and early evening candlelight tours. The Preservation Society of Charleston, Box 521, Charleston (803-722-4630) sponsors similar tours in October.

Magnolia Plantation, Route 61, Charleston (803-571-1266). Open all year. Canoe and bicycle rentals, gift shop, restaurant. Admission charge.

Middleton Place, Route 61, Charleston (803-556-6020). Gardens and stableyards open daily May through February. The house is open all year. Admission charge.

Nathaniel Russell House, 51 Meeting Street, Charleston (803-722-3405). Open every day except Christmas day. The admission charge also includes a tour of the Edmondston-Alston House, 21 East Battery.

Tennessee

Belle Meade, Harding Road, Nashville (615-352-7350). Open every day except Thanksgiving, Christmas and New Year's days. The admission charge includes the 1793 Dunham Station log cabin and the carriage house stable.

Cragfont, Route 25, Gallatin (615-452-7070). Open daily except Monday, April through November, or by appointment. Admission charge.

The Hermitage, Nashville (615-889-2941). Open daily except Christmas Day. Handicapped facilities. Admission charge includes the 1836 Tulip Grove.

Andrew Johnson National Historic Site, Depot and College Streets, Greeneville (615-638-3551). The Visitor Center, the Johnson Home, the president's grave and the park area are all free. A small charge is made for the nearby Johnson Homestead. The Site is open every day except Christmas Day..

Oaklands, North Maney Avenue, Murfreesboro (615-893-0022). Open every day except Monday, Thanksgiving, Christmas and New Year's days. Admission charge.

James K. Polk Home, 301 West Seventh Street, Columbia (615-388-2354). Open every day except Thanksgiving, Christmas and New Year's day. Admission includes adjacent 1816 building formerly owned by the president's sisters, the gardens and the visitor center.

Travellers' Rest, Farrell Parkway, Nashville (615-832-2962). Open every day except Christmas and New Year's days. Weaving house demonstration daily April through October.

Texas

Ashton Villa, 2328 Broadway, Galveston (409-762-3933). Open daily except Thanksgiving and Christmas days. Admission charge includes a documentary film on the 1900 hurricane and its aftermath as well as an 1890s doll house.

Governor's Mansion, 1010 Colorado, Austin (512-475-2121). Open Monday through Friday except state holidays and special occasions. Handicapped facilities. Tours. Free.

House of the Seasons, Jefferson (214-665-8880). Open every day except Thanksgiving and Christmas days. Admission charge includes a guided tour.

Howard-Dickinson House, 501 South Main Street, Henderson (214-657-2925). Open Sundays and by appointment. Admission charge.

Magoffin Home, 1120 Magoffin Avenue, El Paso (915-533-5147. Open daily. Handicapped facilities. Admission charge.

Neill-Cochran House, 2310 San Gabriel, Austin (512-478-2335). Open Wednesday through Sunday except holidays. Admission charge.

Sidbury House, 1609 Chaparral, Corpus Christi (512-883-9352). Open Tuesday through Thursday except holidays. Free.

Steves Homestead, 509 King William Street, San Antonio. Open every day except Thanksgiving, Christmas and New Year's days. Admission charge includes a guided tour.

Virginia

Ash Lawn, Route 795, Charlottesville (804-293-9539). Open every day except Thanksgiving, Christmas and New Year's days. Handicapped facilities. Admission charge includes guided tours and seasonal events.

Appomattox Court House National Historic Park, P.O. Box 218, Appomattox (804-352-8782). Open daily except major holidays. Handicapped facilities. The 1,326-acre park contains original and restored buildings. A self-guided tour begins with a slide presentation at the Visitor Center. The fee is $1 per car.

Belmont, 224 Washington Street, Fredericksburg (703-373-3634). Open daily except Tuesday and Thursday, Christmas and New Year's days. The house contains a gallery of the work of artist Gari Melchers. Admission charge.

Berkeley Plantation, Route 5, Charles City (804-795-2453). Open daily. Admission charge.

Chatham Manor, Fredericksburg (703-373-4461). Open daily except Christmas and New Year's days. Free.

Monticello, Route 53, Charlottesville (804-295-8181). Open every day except Christmas Day. Admission charge.

Mount Vernon, Mount Vernon Memorial Highway, Mount Vernon. Open daily except major holidays. Admission charge.

Norfolk Botanical Gardens, Azalea Garden Road, Norfolk (804-853-6972). Open every day except Christmas and New Year's days. Handicapped facilities. Admission charge, with combination ticket, includes a boat ride and train tours.

Oatlands, U.S. 15, Leesburg (703-777-3174). Open daily from April through mid-December. Admission charge includes special events such as daily races and horse shows.

Sherwood Forest, Route 5, Richmond (804-829-5377). Grounds open daily except Christmas Day. House by appointment only. Admission charge.

Shirley Plantation, Route 5, Richmond (804-795-2385). Open daily except Christmas Day. Admission charge.

Swannanoa, Route 250, Waynesboro. Open daily. Admission charge for palace and gardens or gardens only.

Woodrow Wilson Birthplace, 24 North Coalter Street, Staunton (703-885-0897). Open daily, closed Sunday, December through February and Thanksgiving, Christmas and New Year's days. Admission charge includes a 20-minute film.

Previous page and left: the back porch of President John Tyler's home, Sherwood Forest, in Charles City County, Virginia. The ballroom (below) was part of Tyler's 1790 renovation, and was designed for dancing the Virginia reel. The book on the desk (bottom left) is the only remaining copy of America's first book of law, drawn up by Virginia's House of Burgesses. Bottom: the family breakfast table, holding the President's lap desk and his personal record book.

The sitting room (facing page) of President James Monroe's country home, Ash Lawn, in Charlottesville, Virginia, is part of a plan drawn up by another president, Thomas Jefferson. The 550-acre working plantation is open to the public under the supervision of the College of William and Mary.

Right: a portrait of James Monroe, the fifth president, hangs over a reconstruction of his desk in his Charlottesville home, and (bottom right) his statue graces the grounds. The plantation house (far right), which he called his "cabin castle," became his country home in 1799. Tours today include demonstrations of weaving and spinning (below). Monroe's two daughters, Eliza and Maria Hester, used the crib in the children's room (bottom center).

Often described as one of the most "comfortable" homes anywhere in the United States, Thomas Jefferson's Monticello (these pages) at Charlottesville, Virginia, is also one of the most beautiful, from the great entrance hall (left) to the study (top left) and the parlor (top right) to the magnificent grounds, all of which were carefully and lovingly designed by the third president himself.

When he retired as president, George Washington said that he would spend the rest of his life in "rural amusement" at his beloved Mount Vernon (facing page top), on the banks of the Potomac in Virginia. His retirement was busier than predicted, but he spent long hours there and enjoyed many a meal in the mansion's small dining room (facing page bottom). Woodrow Wilson, the 28th president, was born in the Presbyterian parsonage (this page) at Staunton, Virginia, which has been restored to include a museum which displays his own desk (above).

The marble palace called Swannanoa (these pages), near Waynesboro, Virginia, is a tribute to the art, science and philosophy of Walter and Lao Russell. Created by Mrs. Russell, the Italian Renaissance building is surrounded by magnificent gardens and sculpture and features a window designed by Louis Comfort Tiffany (facing page top right) overlooking the magnificent marble stairway (above).

Oatlands (these pages), near Leesburg, Virginia, was built in the early 19th century by George Carter. Now a property of the National Trust for Historic Preservation, it is open to the public and may be toured from early spring until late fall. From the main hall (facing page bottom), through the breakfast room (above), the library (left), the dining room (facing page top right) and the master bedroom (facing page top left), the house brings back memories of its builder, who also designed the formal gardens (above left).

The Georgian Chatham Manor (these pages) was the seat of a 1,300-acre plantation built near Fredericksburg, Virginia, by William Fitzhugh between 1768 and 1771. The house and outbuildings, set on 30 beautifully-landscaped acres, is open to the public under the direction of the National Park Service. In its early years, Chatham was often visited by George Washington, and during the Civil War President Lincoln came here to confer with his military commanders whose headquarters were in the house.

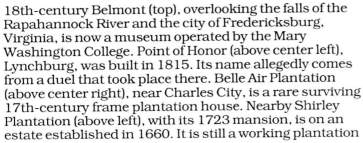

18th-century Belmont (top), overlooking the falls of the Rapahannock River and the city of Fredericksburg, Virginia, is now a museum operated by the Mary Washington College. Point of Honor (above center left), Lynchburg, was built in 1815. Its name allegedly comes from a duel that took place there. Belle Air Plantation (above center right), near Charles City, is a rare surviving 17th-century frame plantation house. Nearby Shirley Plantation (above left), with its 1723 mansion, is on an estate established in 1660. It is still a working plantation operated by the 9th and 10th generations of Hills and Carters. The 1752 house at Kenmore (above right) in Fredericksburg was built by Fielding and Betty Washington Lewis, only sister of George Washington. Berkeley Plantation (facing page), Virginia, is the ancestral home of President William Henry Harrison, who was born here, and his grandson, Benjamin Harrison. The mansion was built in 1726 on the estate that had been acquired by the Harrison family in 1691. The boxwood garden was designed by Benjamin Harrison IV, who built the house.

The portico of Doric columns, suggested by Thomas Jefferson, was added to James Madison's home, Montpelier (far right), Virginia, soon after he married the beautiful Dolley Payne Todd. On April 9, 1865, Robert E. Lee surrendered his troops to Ulysses S. Grant at Appomattox Court House, Virginia. The reconstruction (right and bottom) of the original 1846 building is a monument to the event set in Appomattox National Historical Park (remaining pictures). The 1819 kitchen (below) of the Clover Hill Tavern is now a bookstore. The Mariah Wright House (below right) was built in about 1825 and the home of court clerk George Peers (below far right), in 1850. Isbell House (bottom right) was the home of Thomas Bocock, speaker of the Confederate House of Representatives.

The Norfolk Botanical Gardens (these pages and overleaf), Virginia, were begun in 1936 as a project of the Federal Works Progress Administration. Today they include over 200,000 azaleas, 700 varieties of camellias and 150 rhododendron varieties. The 11 heroic sculptures are of pre-20th century painters. The gardens include a rose collection, a Japanese garden and a fragrance garden for the blind.

Cassius Marcellus Clay, who became minister to Russia, built the brick Italianate White Hall (this page) at Richmond, Kentucky, in 1799. The house, open to the public, has three stories on five levels. The beautiful Greek Revival Ward Hall (facing page) at Georgetown, Kentucky, was built in 1853 by cotton planter Junius Ward. It was recently opened to the public by its present owners who have furnished it with their own family heirlooms.

Ashland (below and right), the Lexington, Kentucky, estate of Henry Clay, who served in the Federal Government for more than 40 years until his death in 1852, includes a 20-room brick Italianate mansion with its original furnishings intact. Locust Grove (bottom and bottom center), near Louisville, is a 1790 Georgian house that was the home of George Rogers Clark, the western military leader of the Revolutionary War. Walnut Hall (bottom right), built in 1842, stands in the Kentucky bluegrass region near Lexington.

The Greek Revival Waveland (this page), near Lexington, Kentucky, was built in 1845. Seven of its 14 rooms are open as a museum and its landscaped grounds are a tract of land once owned by frontiersman Daniel Boone. Liberty Hall (facing page top), in Frankfort, built in 1796, is an outstanding example of Federal architecture. It was built for John Brown, one of Kentucky's first two senators. The antebellum house called Mt. Brilliant (facing page bottom) near Lexington is still part of a working farm.

Farmington (facing page), in Louisville, Kentucky, is an early-19th-century example of a style called Jeffersonian Classical, a pioneer adaptation of Thomas Jefferson's ideas. "My Old Kentucky Home" (this page) in Bardstown is an 1818 home formally known as Federal Hill. Stephen Foster visited there in 1852 and wrote his famous song about it. It is furnished as it was when the composer fell in love with it.

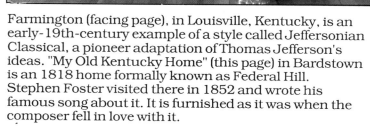

The family home of President Zachary Taylor, Springfield (these pages), Kentucky, was built in 1790 to resemble a Virginia plantation house. Though altered over the years, it has been restored and contains many original furnishings. It is privately owned today.

The Hermitage (this page) was built in 1819 by the hero of the battle of New Orleans and future president of the United States, Andrew Jackson. The house, which is maintained exactly as it was when he died there in 1845, is one of Nashville, Tennessee's most popular visitor attractions. One of the first brick houses in Columbia, Tennessee, was built in 1816 by the father of the 11th president, James Knox Polk. It has been restored as a museum (facing page).

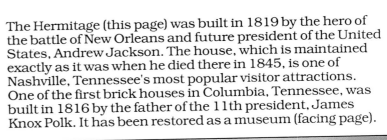

The great Greek-Revival Belle Meade (far left, below and bottom) in Nashville, Tennesee, was completed in 1853 and was one of America's greatest thoroughbred horse breeding farms for nearly 70 years. Its restored interiors and its grounds are open to the public. Carnton (left, bottom left and bottom center), built in 1826 at Franklin, Tennessee, incorporates Federal, Greek Revival and Victorian elements. The grounds, which once contained some of the South's most outstanding gardens, are the final resting place for 1,481 Confederate soldiers who fell at the Battle of Franklin.

The Andrew Johnson National Historic Site (these pages) in Greeneville, Tennessee, includes the house (bottom) the future 17th president bought in 1831, the front of which became his tailor shop. Twenty years later he bought a larger house (below and facing page top) nearby, which was his home for the rest of his life. He remodelled it in 1869, adding the rear porches and the second story to the ell. Both houses have been restored with period furnishings.

Cragfont (top), near Gallatin, Tennessee, was built of stone in the shape of a cross by General James Winchester, a founder of Memphis. The tall Corinthian columns gracing the facade of Rippavilla (facing page top) near Spring Hill, Tennessee, would make the house seem right at home in the Italian Veneto. Two Rivers (left), the 1859 Italianate mansion of David H. McGavock in Nashville, Tennessee, is now a museum. Also in Nashville is Travellers' Rest (above), once the home of Judge John Overton, a confidant of Andrew Jackson. Ferguson Hall (facing page bottom) near Spring Hill, originally the home of a doctor, became part of the Tennessee Orphans' Home.

Oaklands (this page), in Murfreesboro, Tennessee, was expanded from a two-room house during the 1820s. Beautifully-furnished, it is open to the public. Rattle and Snap (facing page top left), near Columbia, Tennessee, is one of America's best examples of elaborate Greek Revival architecture. Vine Hill (facing page top right), in the same area, is an 1836 farmhouse lovingly maintained. After a time as a country club, Myles Manor in Franklin (facing page center right) is now a private home. Franklin's Riverview (facing page bottom) was first in town with indoor plumbing.

Orton Plantation (these pages), near Wilmington, North Carolina, was established in 1725 by Roger Moore, who built the original house with fortress-like walls three feet thick. Wings added in 1910 enhance the antebellum setting of the gardens, whose tree-shaded walks are ablaze with the colors of azaleas, wisteria and other flowering plants from early March. The show continues through late September with crepe myrtle, waterlilies and summer annuals. The gardens are open to the public from March through November.

Biltmore (these pages), the 1895 château and estate of George W. Vanderbilt in Asheville, North Carolina, was designed by Richard Morris Hunt, the architect of New York's Metropolitan Museum and landscaped by Frederick Law Olmsted, designer of New York's Central Park. Vanderbilt's plan for the 12,000-acre estate was to make it entirely self-sufficient with farms, herds and forests. His work in forest conservation set new standards that are still followed. The estate is open to the public, and features a fully-operational winery whose facilities may be toured and products sampled and purchased.

The Wilmington, North Carolina, Azalea Festival, now in its fourth decade, is an annual tribute to the April abundance of azaleas (right). It includes visits to the gardens of houses like Greek Revival Tannahill (left and bottom center) and the charming house on Oleander Drive (bottom left) that is the traditional setting for the official portrait of the Azalea Festival Queen. The charming Jones House (below), near the Tryon Palace complex in New Bern, makes a side trip from the Festival rewarding, as does the Cameron-Hollman House (bottom) in downtown Wilmington.

Among the gardens on the Wilmington Festival tour is the display (top, above left, left and facing page bottom) of some 500 azaleas around a house on Fairway Drive. One of the houses (above) offers a pond stocked with fish. But don't linger too long, you might miss the 10,000 azaleas and 5,000 camellias in the yard over on Forest Hills Drive (facing page top).

Tryon Palace (these pages), in New Bern, North Carolina, was called "the most beautiful building in Colonial America" when it was built as a home for the Royal Governor and the first capitol of the colony. Completely rebuilt in the 1950s, and furnished as it was when it was first built in 1770, the palace and its 13 acres of 18th-century formal gardens are open to the public.

Arlie Gardens (these pages), near Wilmington, North Carolina is part of a 19th-century rice plantation overlooking Wrightsville Sound, where some say Captain Kidd buried his treasure. But the real treasures are the azaleas, the wide lawns, the graceful trees and the peacefulness of the magnificent natural setting of this man-made landscape.

The Historic District of Beaufort (facing page), South Carolina, protects some 170 buildings including many houses like these, whose warm elegance is a textbook definition of the term "Southern hospitality." The Gothic-Revival Rose Hill Plantation (this page) in Beaufort County was begun in the 1850s, but the Civil War and its aftermath prevented completion until nearly a century later. The ceiling above the freestanding staircase (right) is 54 feet high.

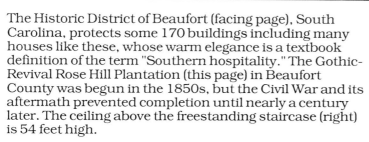

Facing page: (top left, bottom left and bottom right) mansions on South Battery, in Charleston, South Carolina, the homes of merchants and planters in the 18th century, when this was the wealthiest and largest city south of Philadelphia. The house on Bull Street (facing page top right) is one of over 1,000 structures in Charleston's Historic District. Middleton Place (facing page center and this page), near Charleston, is a restored section of a manor house begun in 1741. Its landscaped gardens are the oldest in America. (Photographed at Middleton Place, Charleston, South Carolina.)

Above: Boone Hall Plantation, near Charleston, South Carolina. The 1809 Federal-style Nathaniel Russell House (remaining pictures), now a museum, was the home of one of Charleston's leading merchants. The furnishings and ornamentation are all original. The three-story flying staircase with its Palladian window (left) is one of the city's most impressive architectural treasures.

Magnolia Plantation (these pages), near Charleston, covers over 500 acres with one of the most beautiful informal gardens in the country. The Victorian plantation house is the third on the same site, having replaced the oldest plantation house in the Carolinas. The original garden was begun in about 1680.

The nature trails that wind through Magnolia Gardens (these pages), offer flowering beauty at every turn. They also lead through a waterfowl refuge where over 170 different species of birds have been identified. Visitors may rent bicycles and canoes to vary the birdwatching experience. The Magnolia Plantation house (below) is open and contains exhibits showing plantation life since the Civil War.

The three-quarter-mile allee with its moss-draped live oak trees (top right), planted in 1743 at Boone Hall Plantation (these pages), provides a classic image of the popular view of Southern plantation life. Boone Hall, near Charleston, South Carolina, was established in 1681 as a cotton plantation and restored in 1935. Open to visitors, it is still a working plantation producing pecans and vegetables and farming cattle and sheep.

Cypress Gardens (these pages), north of Charleston, South Carolina, is a 160-acre wonderland of azaleas, cypress trees, camellias and other flowering plants. It is open to visitors all year but it is at its spectacular best in early spring when the azaleas are in bloom. Facing page: knobs rising from the ground near the trunk of a cypress tree allow the tree to supply needed air to its roots submerged under water.

In season, the wonders of Cypress Gardens may be seen from the quiet comfort of a boat, but the pleasure of walking through the azalea-lined trails is also a unique experience. The gardens include a picnic area to help make the pleasure a day-long experience.

The Heyward-Washington House (these pages) (photographs courtesy of the Charleston Museum, Charleston, South Carolina), on Church Street in Charleston, was built in 1770 by planter Daniel Heyward and inherited by his son, Thomas Heyward, a signatory of the Declaration of Independence. It was rented in 1791 for the use of President Washington. Carefully restored, it is now owned by the Charleston Museum and is open to visitors. Top and facing page bottom: the parlour, (above and facing page top) the card room and (left) the front parlour.

The Greek-Revival Wedge Plantation (facing page) near Charleston, South Carolina, was built in 1826, and its gardens contain magnolias planted by the builder. Nearby Drayton Hall (top) (a property of the National Trust for Historic Preservation) was completed in 1742. It is one of the few houses in the area to have survived both the Revolutionary and Civil wars. The Joseph Manigault House in Charleston (above, above right and right) (photographs courtesy of the Charleston Museum, Charleston, South Carolina), a 1790 Federal-style house with fine Adam details, was designed by the owner's brother, Gabriel. It is believed to be the first house in the city designed by an architect.

The 1730 Georgian Fenwick Hall (top left), on John's Island near Charleston, was used as headquarters by the British during the Revolution and by the Union Army in the Civil War. Lowndes Grove (top) and Hampton Plantation (above left) are both classic antebellum plantation houses as is Harrietta (above and left) on the Santee River. Rose Hill Plantation (facing page), near Union, is part of a state park. It was built for William H. Gist, Governor of South Carolina, who led the state out of the Union in 1860.

When James Oglethorpe established the Georgia colony in 1733, he laid out a city he named Savannah for the Shawnee Indians he found there. His original town plan, the first in America with squares, straight avenues and orderly building lots, was never altered as the city of Savannah grew, giving it a unique appearance. After Eli Whitney invented the cotton gin nearby, the city became a major port whose wealth was reflected in the houses shown on these pages.

The 1793 John Mongan House (far left), once the rectory of Christ Episcopal Church, stands on Warren Square, as do many other fine 18th-century houses (left). Jones Street, the heart of Savannah's biggest redevelopment, offers beautiful examples of mid-19th-century architecture (bottom left), including the Abraham Minis House (below far left). The 18th-century "pink house" (below left) has been converted to a restaurant, and the Andrew Low House (below), where Juliette Gordon Low founded the Girl Scouts of America in 1912, is now a museum. Set among the Victorian houses on Whitefield Square is an occasional reminder of the city's classical elegance (bottom center), and along Oglethorpe Street (bottom) are reminders of the founder's original narrow building lots.

The 1820 Isaiah Davenport House (above left, top and facing page), in Savannah, Georgia, was saved from demolition in 1955 by the Historic Savannah Foundation, which restored it and converted it to a museum exhibiting a fine collection of Chippendale, Hepplewhite and Sheraton furniture. Above left: a bedroom, (facing page top) the parlour, and (facing page bottom) the dining room. The Foundation also restored the home's 18th-century garden. The boyhood home (above right) of President Jimmy Carter in Archery, near Plains, Georgia, was the home of the 39th president between 1928 and 1944, until he entered the U.S. Naval Academy at Annapolis, Maryland.

The Juliette Gordon Low birthplace (these pages), on Bull Street in Savannah, Georgia, has been restored to its 1870 appearance and is a memorial to the founder of the Girl Scouts of America. The Regency-style house was built in 1818 for James M. Wayne, Savannah's mayor. He sold it to his niece and her husband, the parents of the future Mrs. Low, who was born in the house on Halloween in 1860. The house is now a national program center for Girl Scouts as well as a beautifully-furnished restoration.

The 1885 Queen-Anne-style Lapham-Patterson House (facing page) in Thomasville, Georgia, has an unusual polygonal porch as well as stained glass and intricate decorative woodwork. Susina Plantation (top and above), west of Beachton, is a restored 1841 Greek-Revival house. Greenwood Plantation (left), near Thomasville, is an altered pioneer house with modifications by architect Stanford White.

Pebble Hill (these pages), near Thomasville, Georgia, is the third plantation house on the site. It was designed in 1936 by Abram Garfield, son of President James A. Garfield, who also designed the loggia (bottom) in 1914 for the house's predecessor, later destroyed by fire. The murals in the main drawing room (bottom center left and bottom right), showing local wildlife, were originally a large oil painting, cut to fit. Pebble Hill is open every day for guided tours.

Kingsley Plantation (below) is on Fort George Island, near Jacksonville, Florida. The Robert Gamble Mansion (right, bottom and bottom right) near Tampa is a memorial to Confederate Secretary of State Judah Benjamin. In Jacksonville, the architectural styles range from the bold castellated Check Mansion (far right) to the sheltering Prairie style on Riverside Avenue (below center). More in keeping with the terrain and tradition is the Debray Mansion (bottom center) at Debray.

The 1927 Mediterranean-style Epping Forest (previous pages) was built in Jacksonville, Florida, for Alfred I duPont. John Ringling built his Ca' D'zan (these pages and overleaf) at Sarasota in 1925 following the Venetian tradition, but outdoing the Doges in opulence. The 68-acre estate includes an art museum, a circus museum and an original 18th-century Italian theater.

107

The 1829 Greek-Revival Gorgas House (top, above left and facing page bottom) is one of eight landmarks on the campus of the University of Alabama in Tuscaloosa, as is the 1841 President's Mansion (above right), a brick structure covered with stucco. Oakleigh (facing page top), designed and begun in 1833 by merchant James W. Roper, is now a small museum in the Oakleigh Garden Historic District of Mobile, which contains many other early-19th-century houses along a charming promenade.

The 1820 Kirkbride House, also called the Fort Conde-Charlotte House (right, below and bottom), in Mobile, is said to have been the city's first jail. The Leroy Pope Walker House (below right) in Huntsville features an unusual rooftop lookout point, as does Dean Page Hall (facing page) in Eufaula, one of nearly 100 historic reminders of the city's days at the center of the cotton trade.

Greek-Revival and Italianate styles are mixed in 1853 Sturdivant Hall (left and bottom left), a restored mansion in Selma, Alabama . The oldest house in Birmingham, Alabama, is 1822 Arlington (below, bottom and bottom center). Both houses have been preserved as city museums.

One of Alabama's best Greek Revival homes is Gaineswood (this page) in Demopolis. It was begun ten years after its neighbor, the 1832 Bluff Hall (facing page: top right, top left and bottom left). The cast iron fence and porch of the Richards DAR House in Mobile (facing page: center left, center right and bottom right) add a welcoming touch of charm that continues into its parlor.

115

Springfield (facing page top right and this page bottom) is an 1800 plantation house near Fayette, Mississippi. Waverly (remaining pictures) near West Point, Mississippi, has an identical recessed Ionic loggia in front and back. The stair hall has three tiers of cantilevered octagonal balconies (below). It was built in 1852 and restored in the 1960s.

The fine plasterwork and rich interior details, including those of an elliptical staircase (left) which leads to a ballroom on the second floor, make the Charles McLaran House, Riverview (these pages) one of the most impressive houses in Columbus, Mississippi.

The 1855 Greek-Revival mansion, Dunleith (left, below and bottom left) in Natchez, Mississippi, has an impressive Tuscan portico with cast iron balustraded decks and a suitably elegant interior. Rosalie (bottom center and bottom), also in Natchez, like Dunleith, has matching entrances on the first and second stories.

The 1840 Greek-Revival Cedar Grove (facing page) in Vicksburg, Mississippi, has a two-story front portico and a two-story gallery in the rear with a cast iron stair leading to the garden and its cast iron gazebo and fountain. D'Evereux (top and right), in Natchez, Mississippi, again built in 1840, also has landscaped gardens and terraces. The 1860 Victorian Italianate Longwood (above), near Natchez, is called Nutt's Folly because of its exotic style.

One of the best-preserved of all the Natchez Mississippi plantations, Melrose (these pages), built in 1845, is also handsomely furnished. The beautifully-carved wood panel suspended over the dining room table (above) is an early hand-powered fan installed to help diners keep cool.

Estevan Hall (this page) in Helena, Arkansas, has been continuously occupied by the Hanks family since it was built in 1820. Solid gentility is reflected in the imposing W.W. Case House (facing page top) in Jonesboro and in the equally impressive Horace Franklin Rogers House (facing page bottom) in Fort Smith.

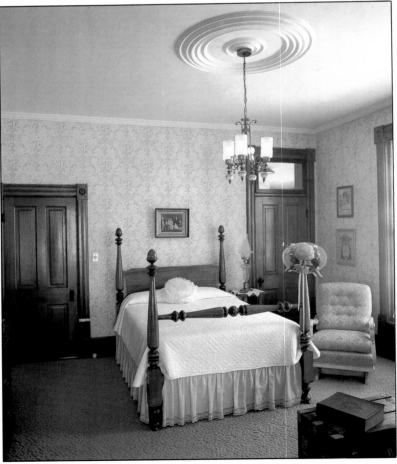

Victorian/Queen Anne Rosalie (top, above, left and facing page) in Eureka Springs, Arkansas, is a model of warm comfort inside and out. More traditional solid comfort is the message of the Galloway House (above left) in Clavendon, Arkansas.

The McCollum-Chidester House (below) in Camden, Arkansas, calls out to you to try the swing on the verandah. And the dogwood tree at the Sanders Garland House (bottom) in Washington, Arkansas, is just as inviting. In Marianna, who could resist this balcony (right)? Or the Victorian charm of Bonneville (bottom center and bottom right) in Fort Smith?

The tower, the verandah, the spindles of the Pillow-Thompson House (above) in Helena, Arkansas, make this one of the best of the Queen-Anne-style houses. The fine Martha Mitchell House (facing page) in Pine Bluff is made even better by the large dogwood tree in front.

Rosedown Plantation (facing page), near Baton Rouge, Louisiana, is maintained, along with its gardens, as a museum. Further down the river, near New Orleans, are the Beauregard House (top), Chretein Point (above and above right), and Steamboat House (right), which looks like it could have made the trip on its own.

San Francisco Plantation (these pages), near Reserve, Louisiana, is a unique mixture of architectural styles. The interior, as charming as the exterior, is furnished as it was when the house was built in 1850. It is open as a museum.

Oak Alley Plantation, at Vacherie, Louisiana (this page and overleaf), takes its name from its avenue of live oak trees that were 100 years old when the house was built in 1850. The house and grounds are open for tours. Ashland-Belle Helene Plantation (facing page top), near Geismar, and Madewood Plantation (facing page bottom) near Napoleonville, Louisiana, are both rare survivors of the Civil War.

Among the great houses of Louisiana are Evergreen (left), just south of Donaldsonville, with its unusual flying staircase; Glencoe (below, bottom and bottom left), a beautifully-furnished wooden palace near Jackson; Bocage Plantation (below center), built in 1831; and L'Hermitage (bottom center), near Darrow.

The 1787 Destrehan Plantation (facing page top) is the oldest plantation house on the lower Mississippi. Houmas House (facing page bottom and left), built in 1840, has been restored and furnished with antiques. Both are open for tours. The Hermann-Grima House (top left, top right and above) in New Orleans is also open.

Ardoyne (previous pages), built in 1900 near Houma, Lousiana, was copied from a picture of a Scottish castle. The Victorian house has 21 rooms, all with 16-foot ceilings. Sixty-four-room Nottoway (these pages) near Baton Rouge, is a pleasing combination of Greek Revival and Italianate architecture, built in 1859. It has been restored and is open to the public.

The homes of Corpus Christi, Texas, are as much a visitor attraction as the wonderful beaches on the nearby Gulf of Mexico. The Yellow House in the Rockport section (facing page top), the Sidbury House (facing page bottom) and the Simon Guggenheim House (below right) are as warm and informal as the environment. But formality is there, too, in houses like Fulton Mansion (bottom left). Further up the coast in Jefferson, plantation houses are built high above the water (below left), and the guardian of the front door of the 1839 Manse (bottom right) keeps his nose alert for the next high tide.

Many of the houses along fashionable Swiss Avenue in Dallas, Texas, are in grand Italianate style (top). More in keeping with the Southern tradition is the Greek-Revival Shriver House in Austin (remaining pictures)

The Aldredge House on Swiss Avenue in Dallas (facing page and above left) was built in 1916. The interior walls are mahogany. Among its neighbors is the Collins House (remaining pictures), a combination of styles with emphasis on the Federal. Many of the houses on the street are open to the public on a spring weekend each year for the benefit of the Swiss Avenue Historic Association.

The House of Seasons (these pages) in Jefferson, Texas, makes good use of its cupola, which can be seen from the center hall (right and above right) or from inside (center right) where colored glass windows give it an unusually happy aspect. The house is furnished with period antiques in the French parlour (above), the parlour (top center), the master bedroom (top right), and the library (far right).

The Howard-Dickinson House (these pages) in Henderson is a classic example of early farm life in East Texas, including the family Bible prominently displayed in the parlor and the Lone Star flag of Texas waving from the front porch. On this visit, the dining room (facing page bottom) is decorated for a wedding, but the welcome latch is always out. It's how they do things in East Texas.

The variety of houses in Texas is as broad as the Lone Star State itself, ranging from the Edward Steves Homestead (facing page) in San Antonio, to Sweetbrush in Austin (below), the Tate-Seuftenberg-Brandon House (bottom) in Columbus, a house (right) on King William Street in San Antonio, and Woodlawn (bottom right) in Austin.

The 1859 Ashton Villa (previous pages) in Galveston, Texas, as wonderful inside as out, is open as a museum. The 1852 Neill-Cochran House (these pages) in Austin, also a museum, has floor-to-ceiling French windows overlooking its Doric portico. The house has two parlors (facing page top and above) and other rooms furnished with valuable antiques.

Among the houses that make Galveston, Texas, so comfortably charming is the Wilbur Cherry House (above). In El Paso, the single story adobe Spanish Colonial Magoffin Homestead (remaining pictures), once the home of the city's mayor, is a U-shaped structure with a central courtyard. It was built in 1875 and later expanded. Facing page: (top) the family parlour, and (bottom) the entrance hall.

The Governor's Mansion (these pages) in Austin, Texas, is the state's second executive mansion, built in 1856. The portrait in the small parlor (right) is of Sam Houston. Facing page top right and center: the conservatory. This Greek Revival house also has a fine Victorian carriage house.

The large dining room (far right) and other rooms in the Texas Governor's Mansion (these pages), Austin, are all welcoming and warm, which is a Texas tradition. They include the conservatory (right), the large parlor (below and bottom center right), the small parlor (bottom center right), and the library (bottom right). Bottom center left: a large pier glass and candelabra in the hall. The Ionic portico (overleaf) has a diamond-patterned balustrade on each level.